GOODNIGHT BATCAVE

by Dave Croatto

●

Pictures by Tom Richmond

In the great gray cave

There were a lot of bats

And souvenirs saved

And the pictures of—

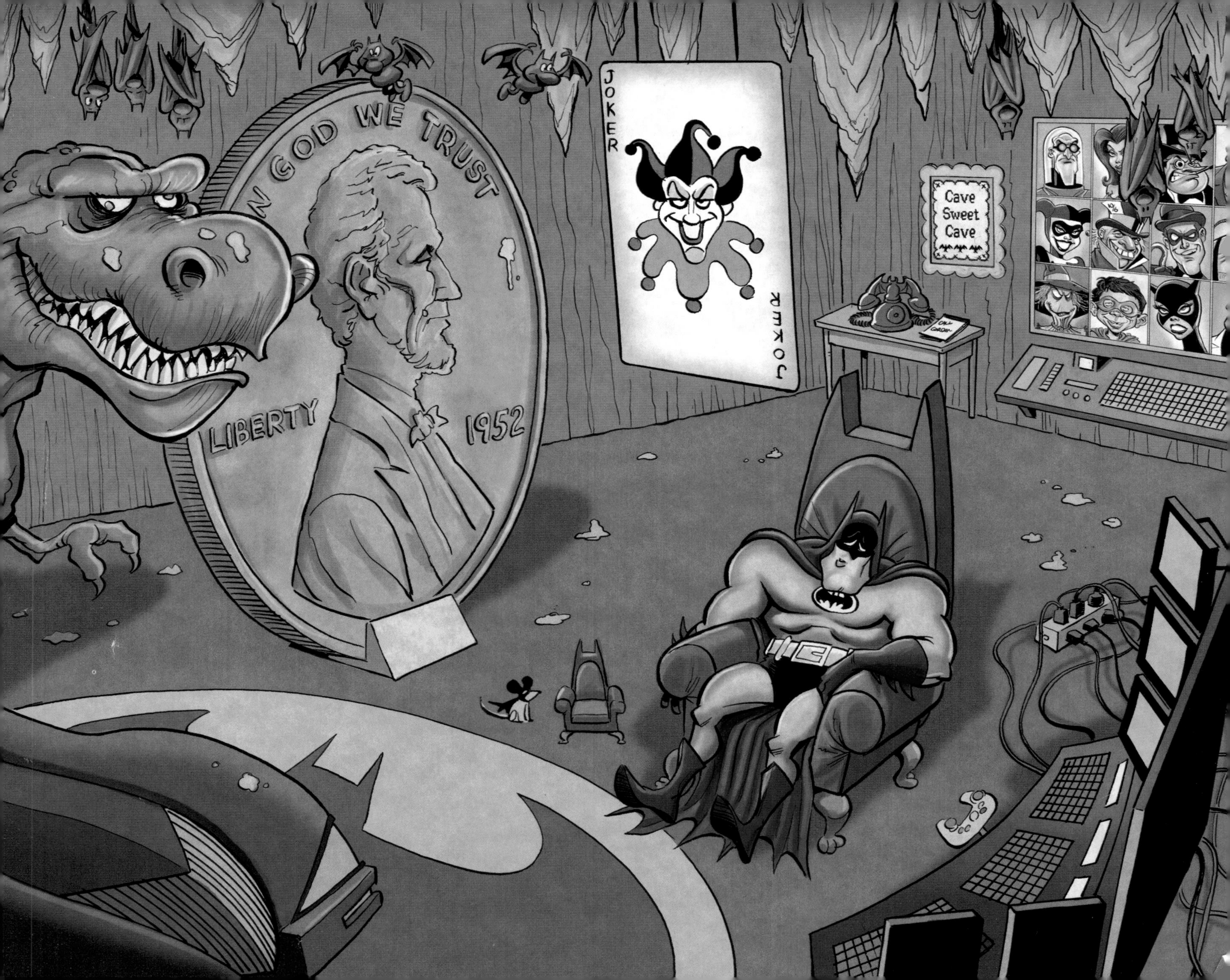N GOD WE TRUST
LIBERTY
1952
JOKER
JOKER
Cave
Sweet
Cave

The rogues who have never behaved

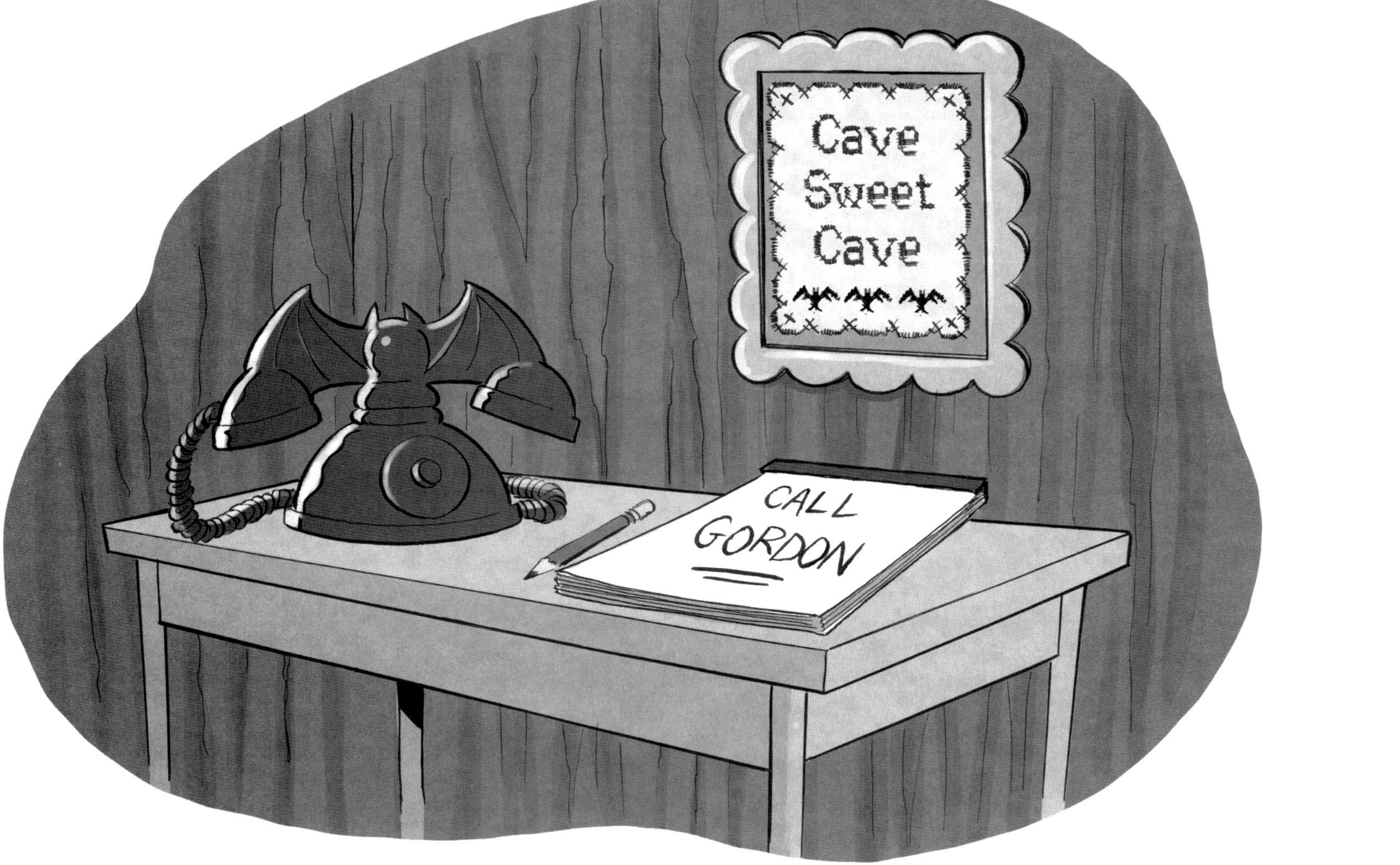
Cave
Sweet
Cave
CALL
GORDON

And there was a special phone and walls of stone

And two comfy Bat-chairs
And some secret stairs

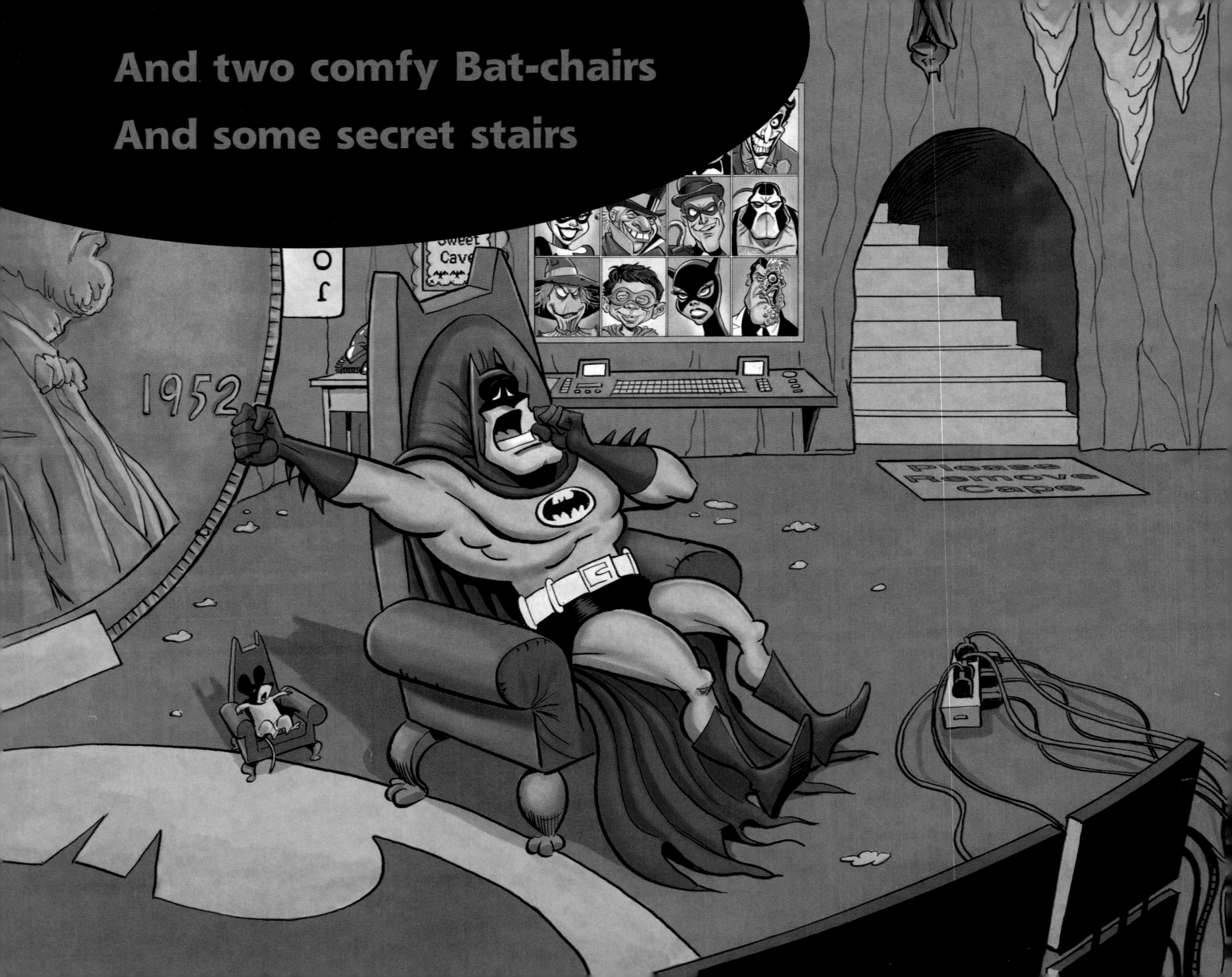
Sweet Cave
1952
Please Remove Cape

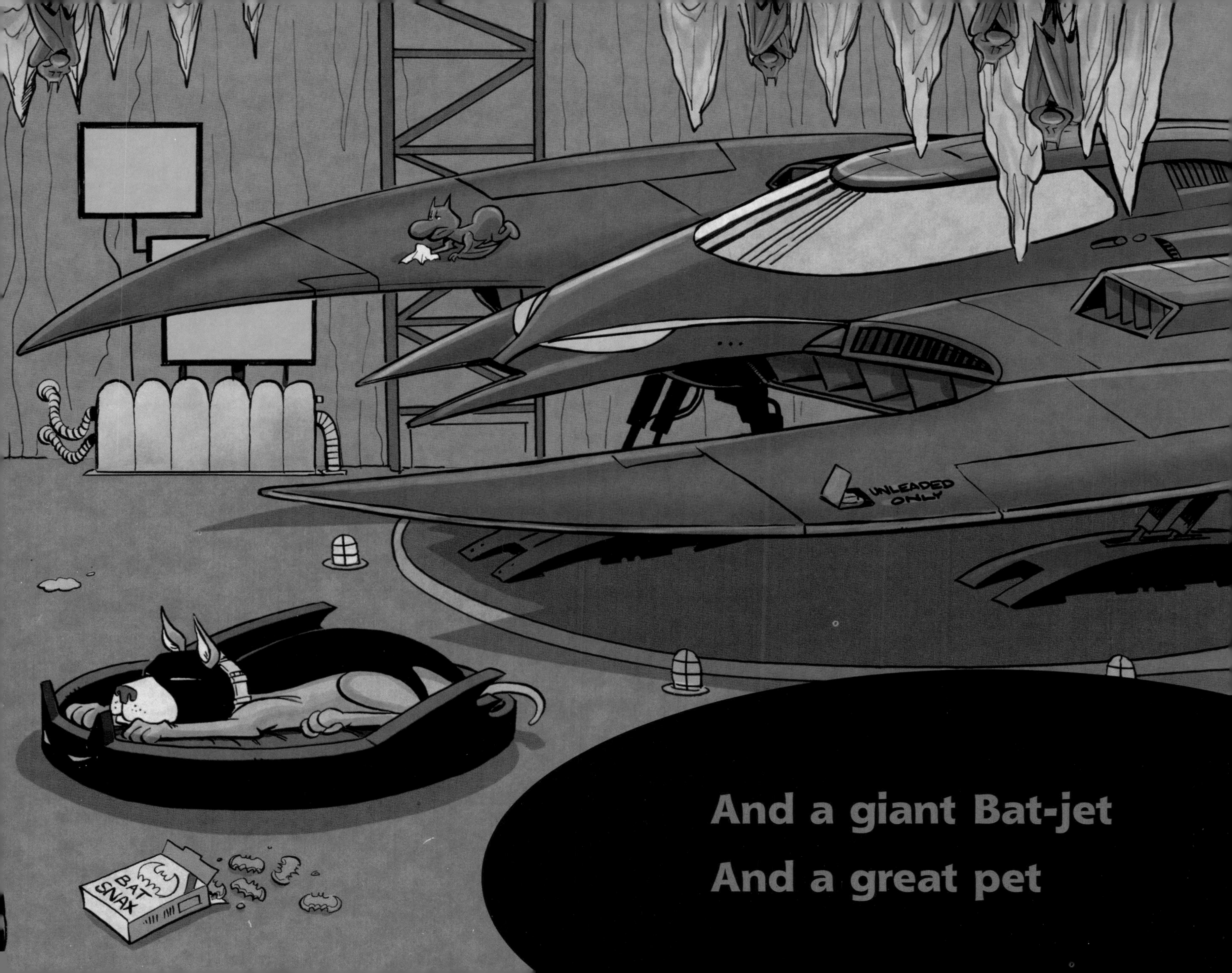
UNLEADED ONLY
BAT SNAX

And a giant Bat-jet
And a great pet

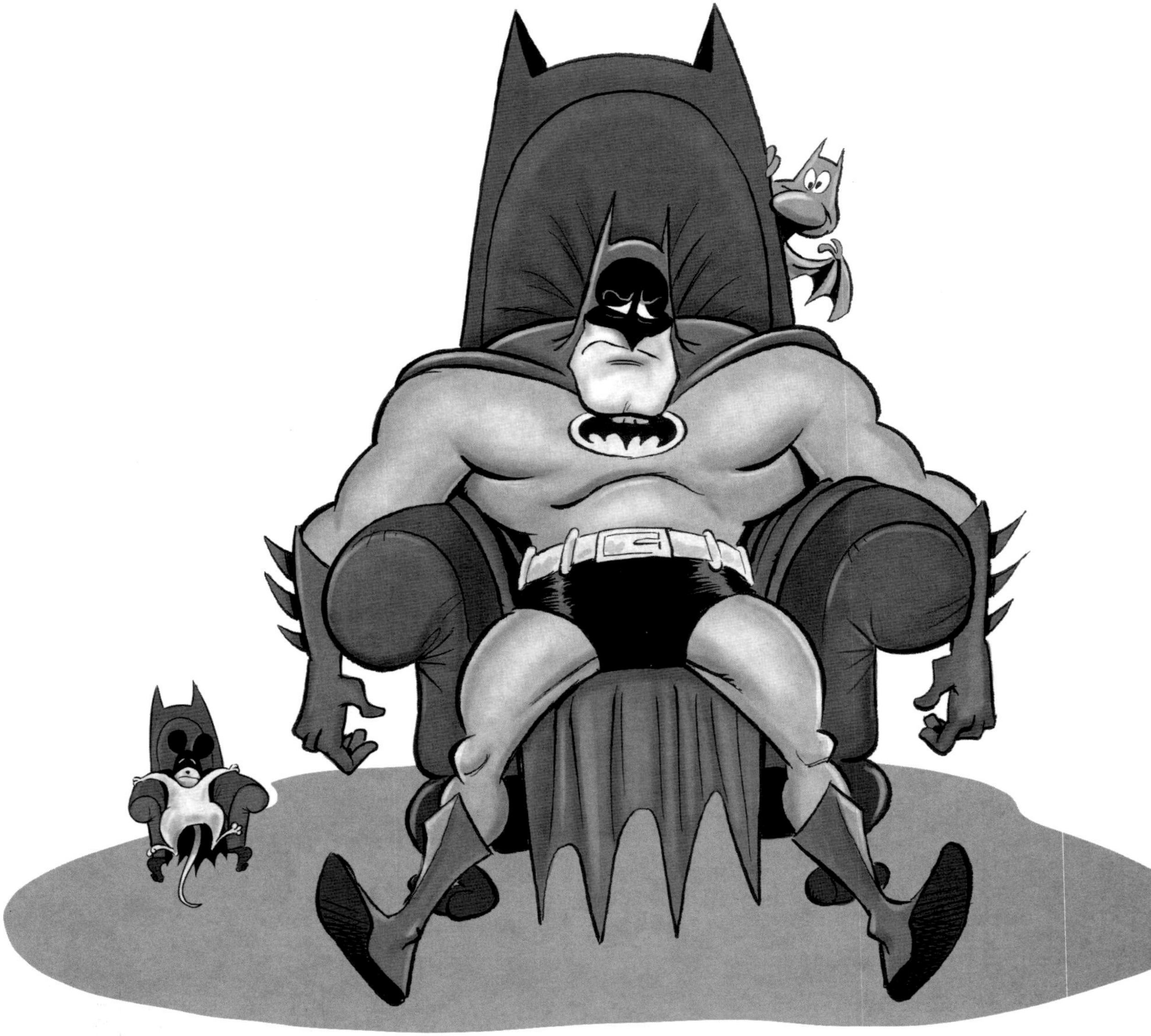

And a cape and cowl and an exhausted scowl

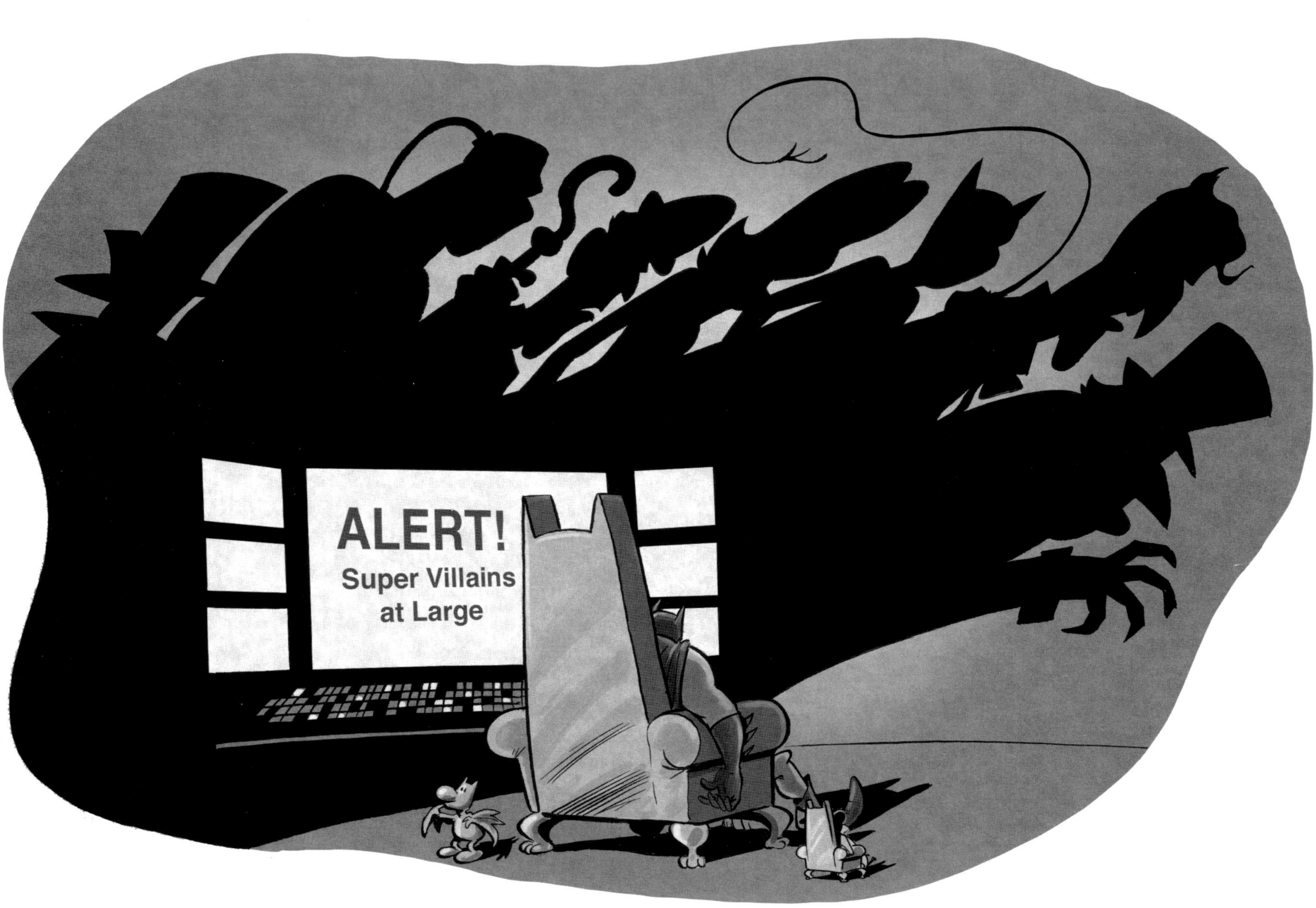
ALERT!
Super Villains at Large

And a gang of crazed villains
Who were there on the prowl!

Goodnight cave

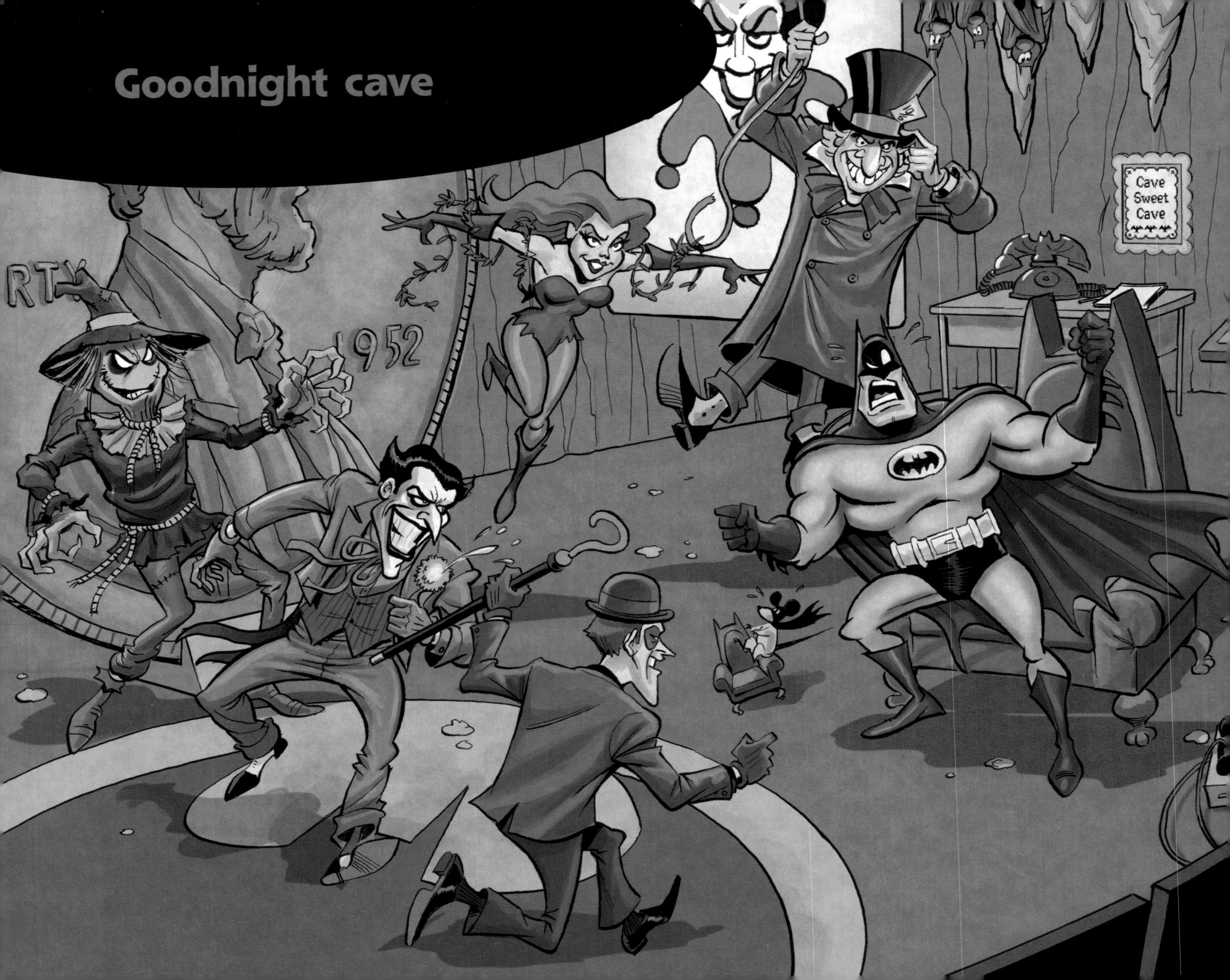
RTY
1952
Cave
Sweet
Cave

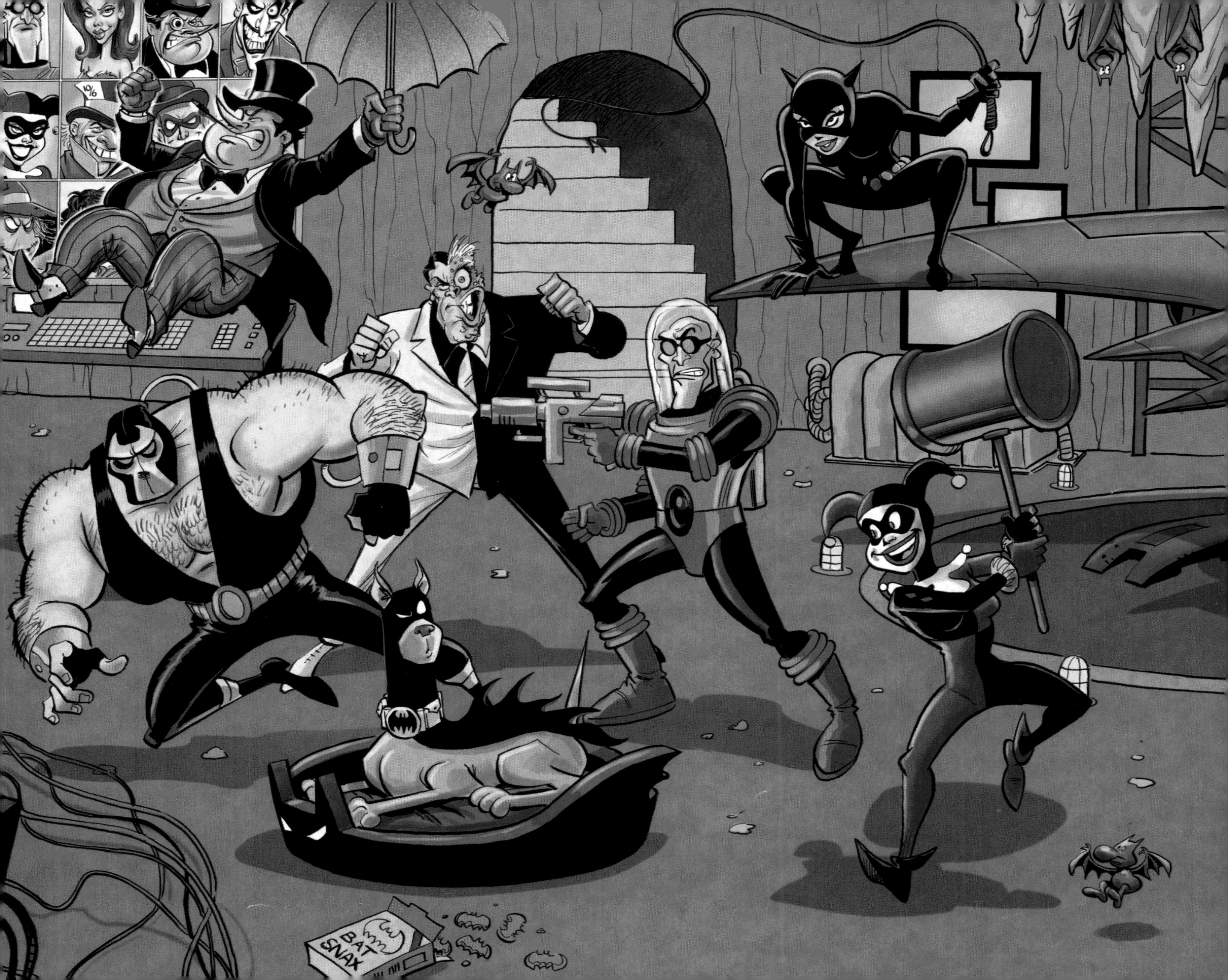
BAT SNAX

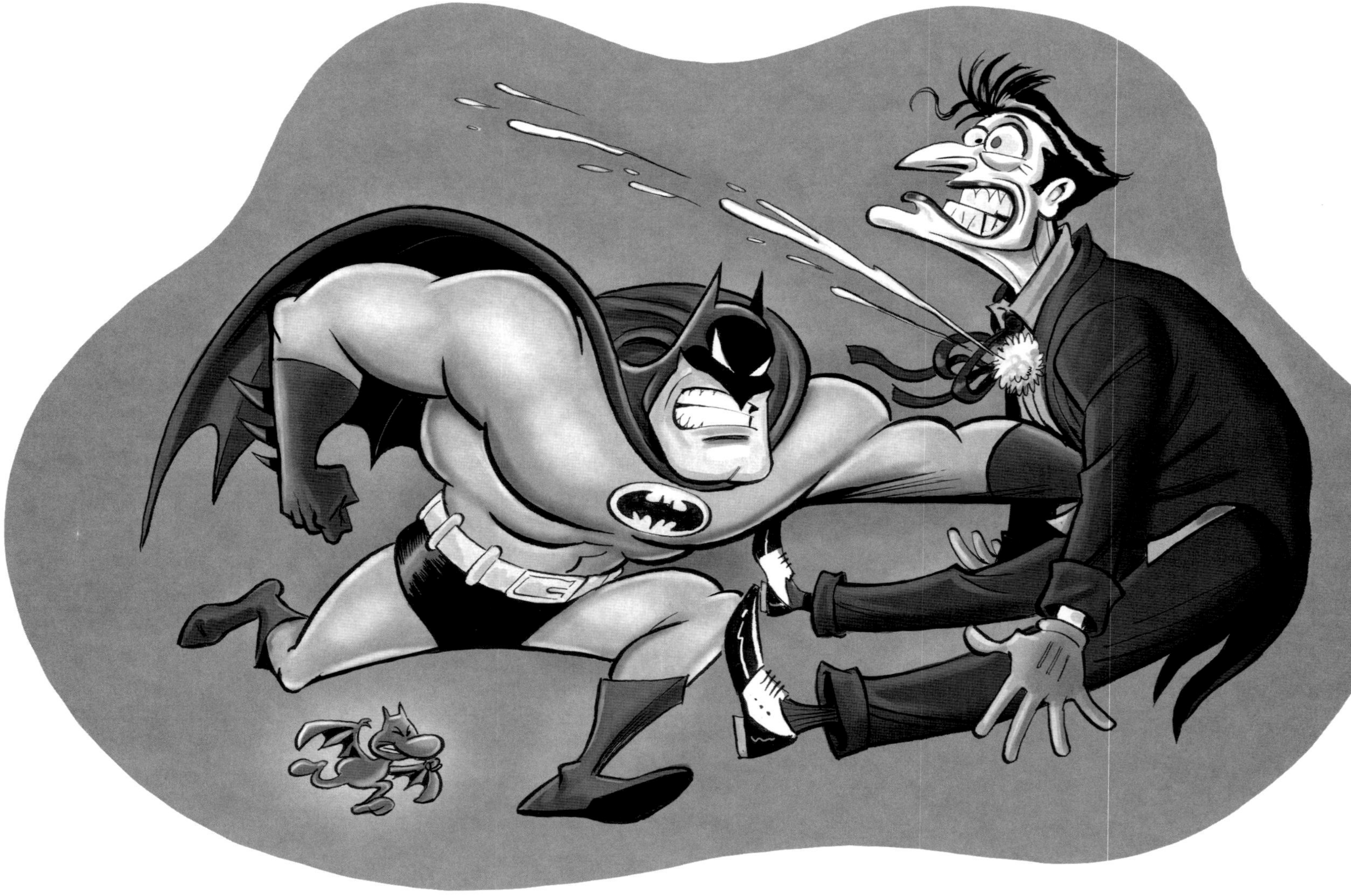

Goodnight knave

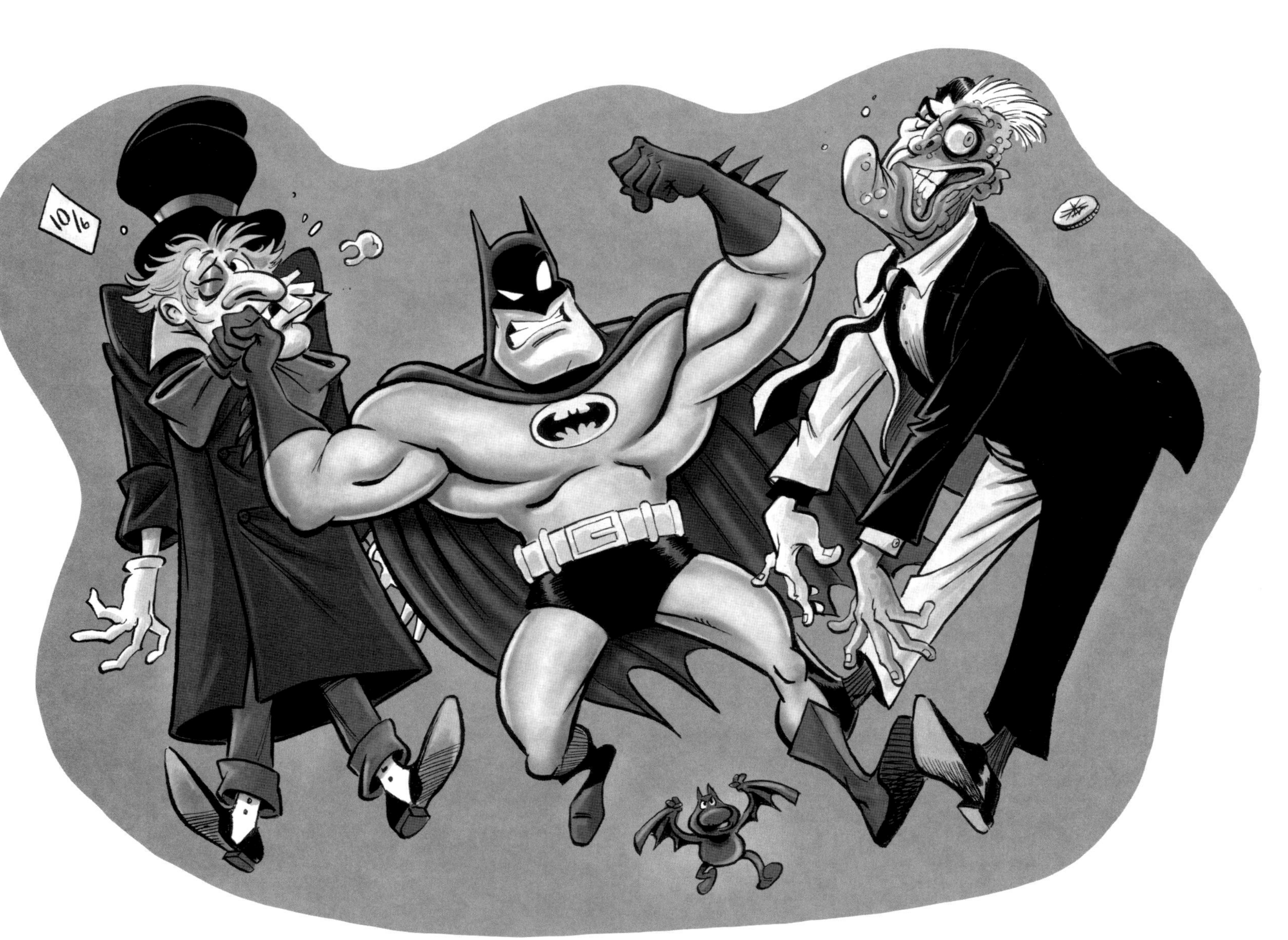
10/6

Goodnight crooks while they rant and they rave

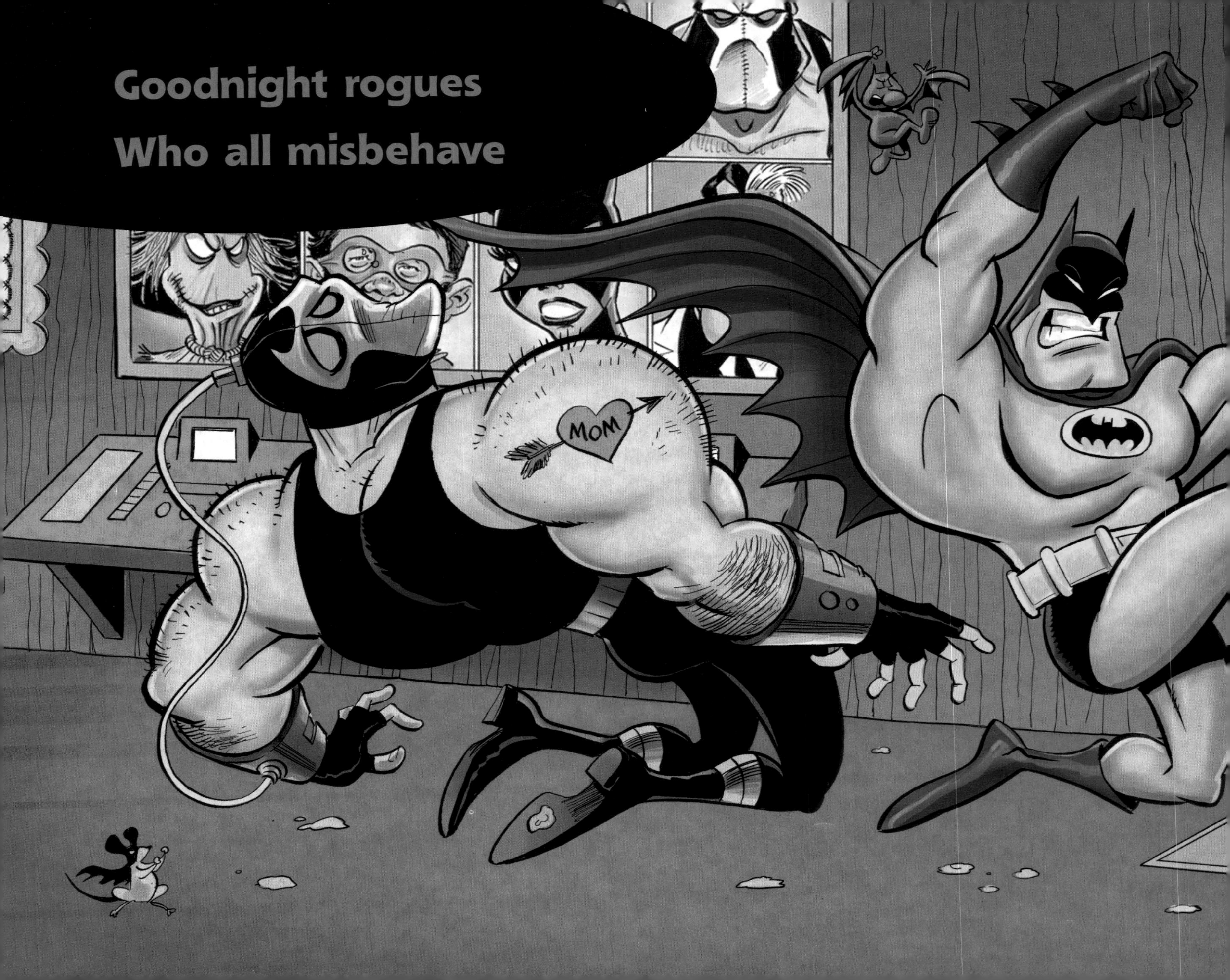
Goodnight rogues
Who all misbehave
MOM

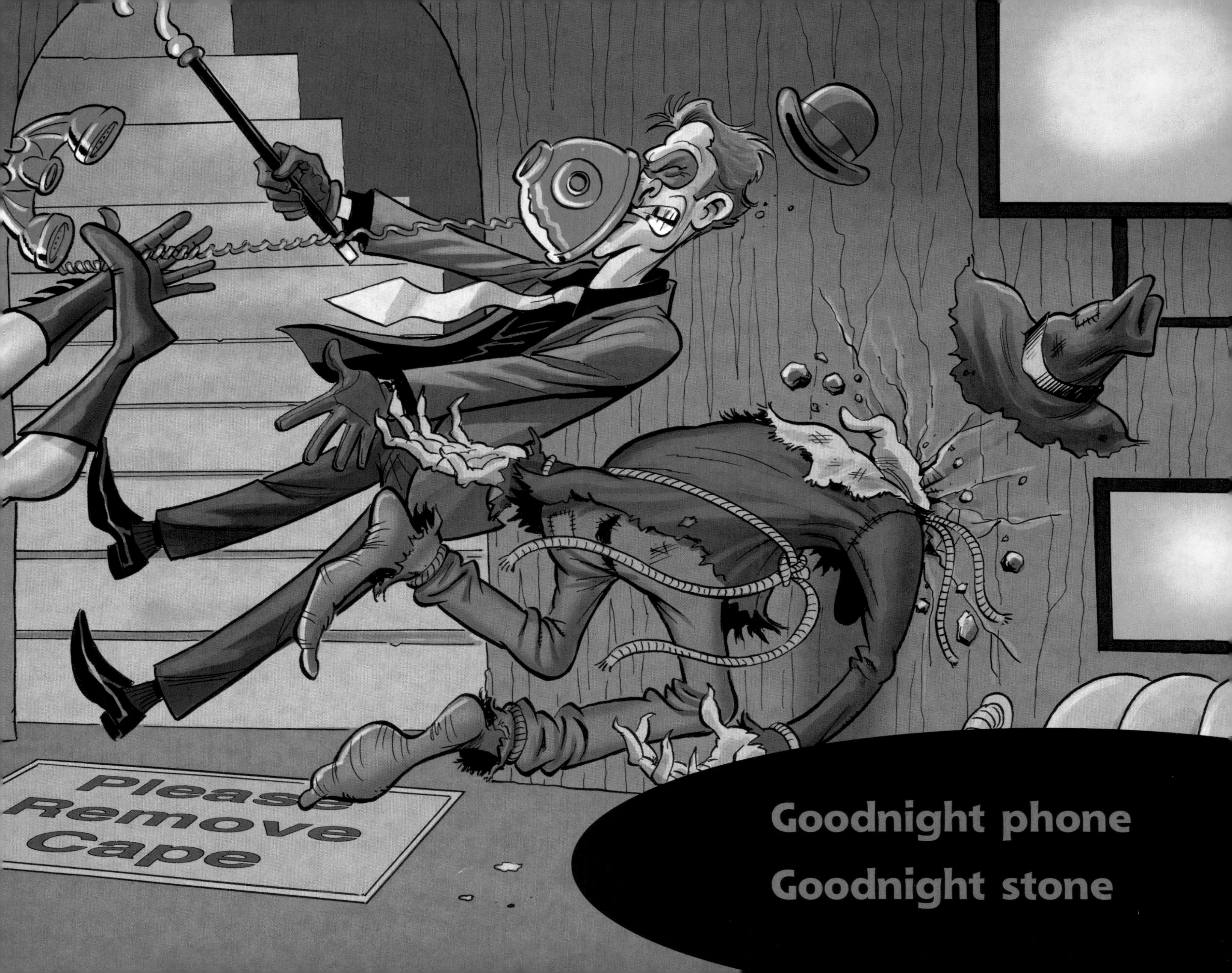
Please
Remove
Cape

Goodnight phone
Goodnight stone

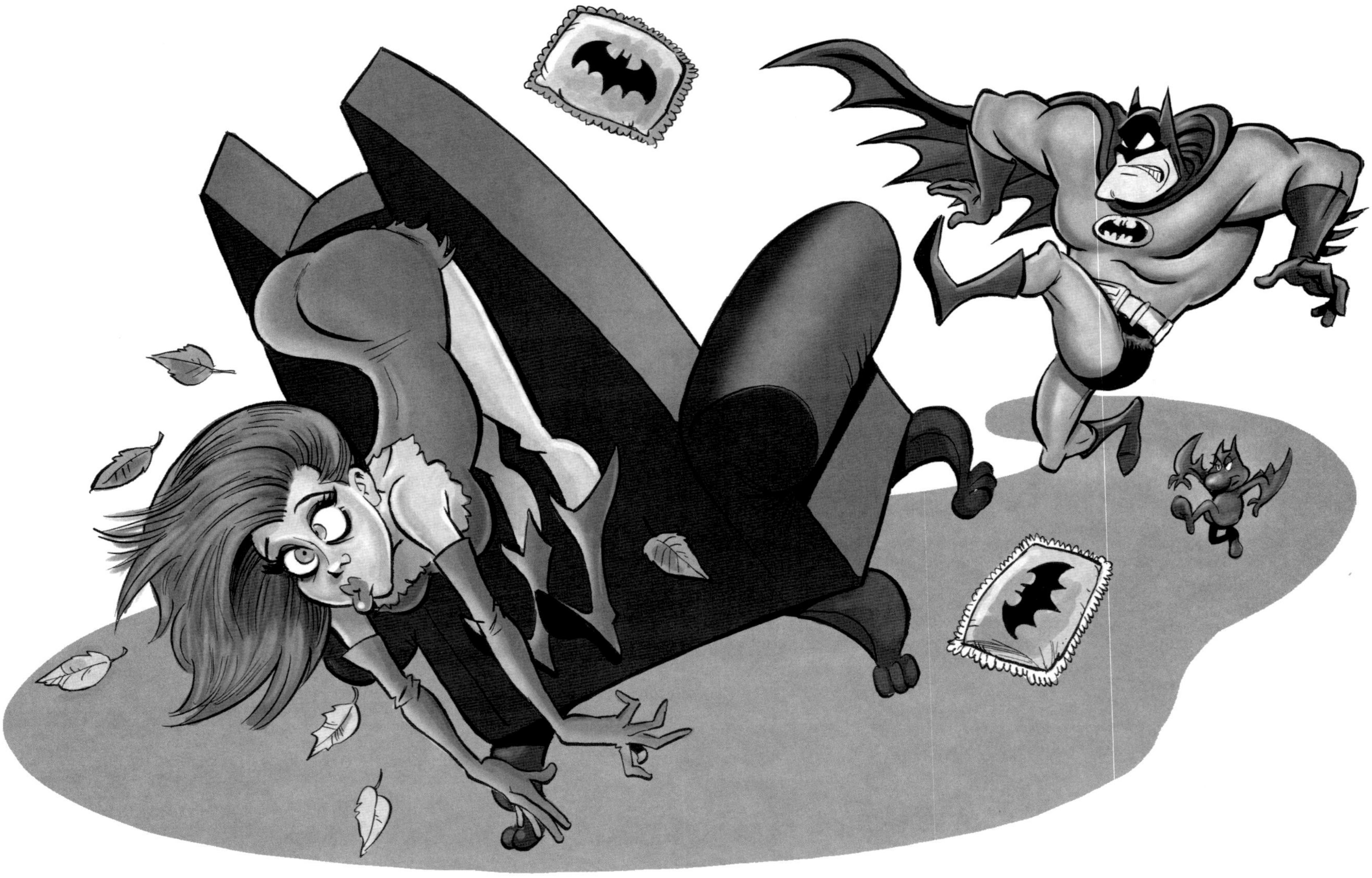

Goodnight Bat-chairs

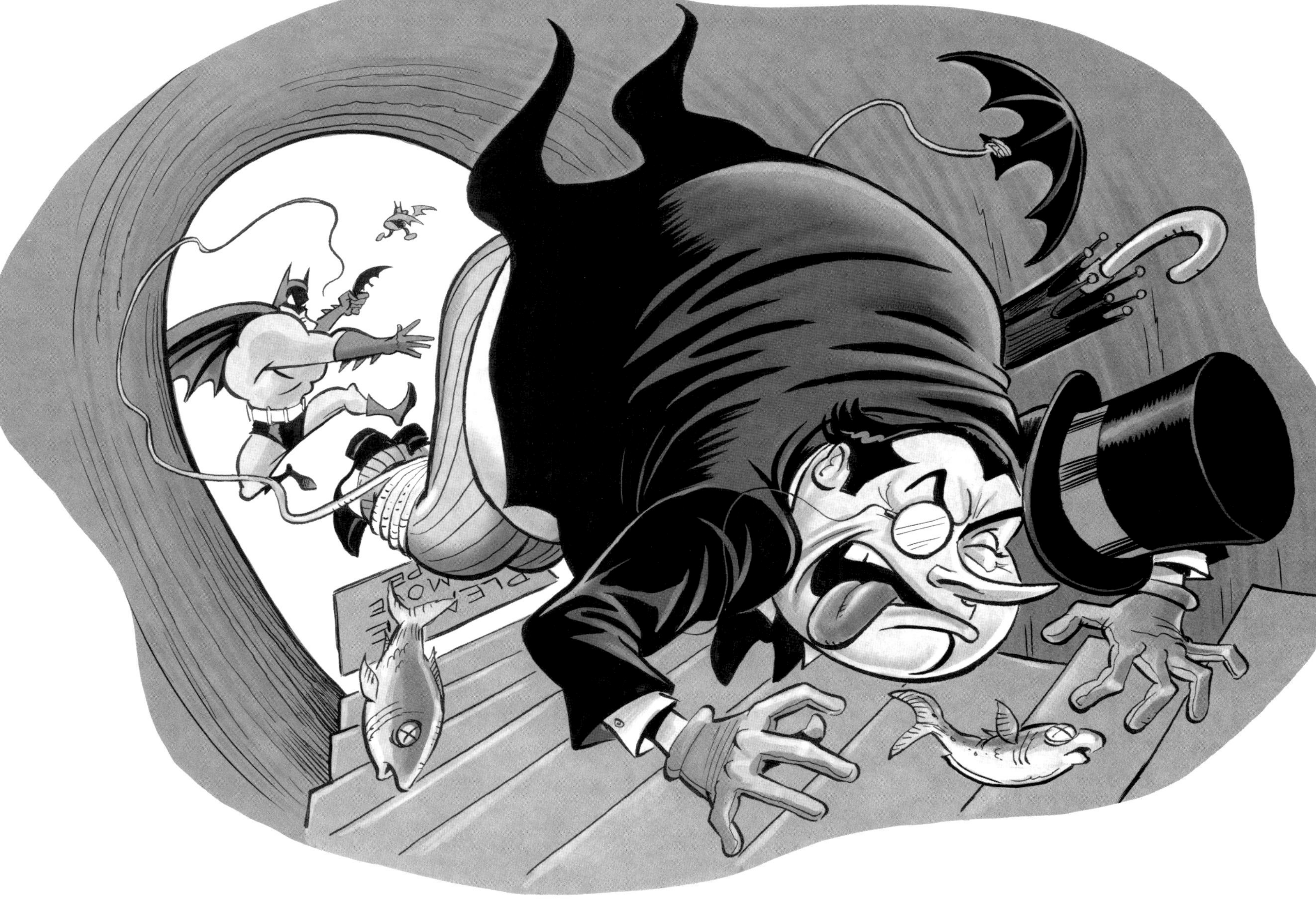

And goodnight Bat-stairs

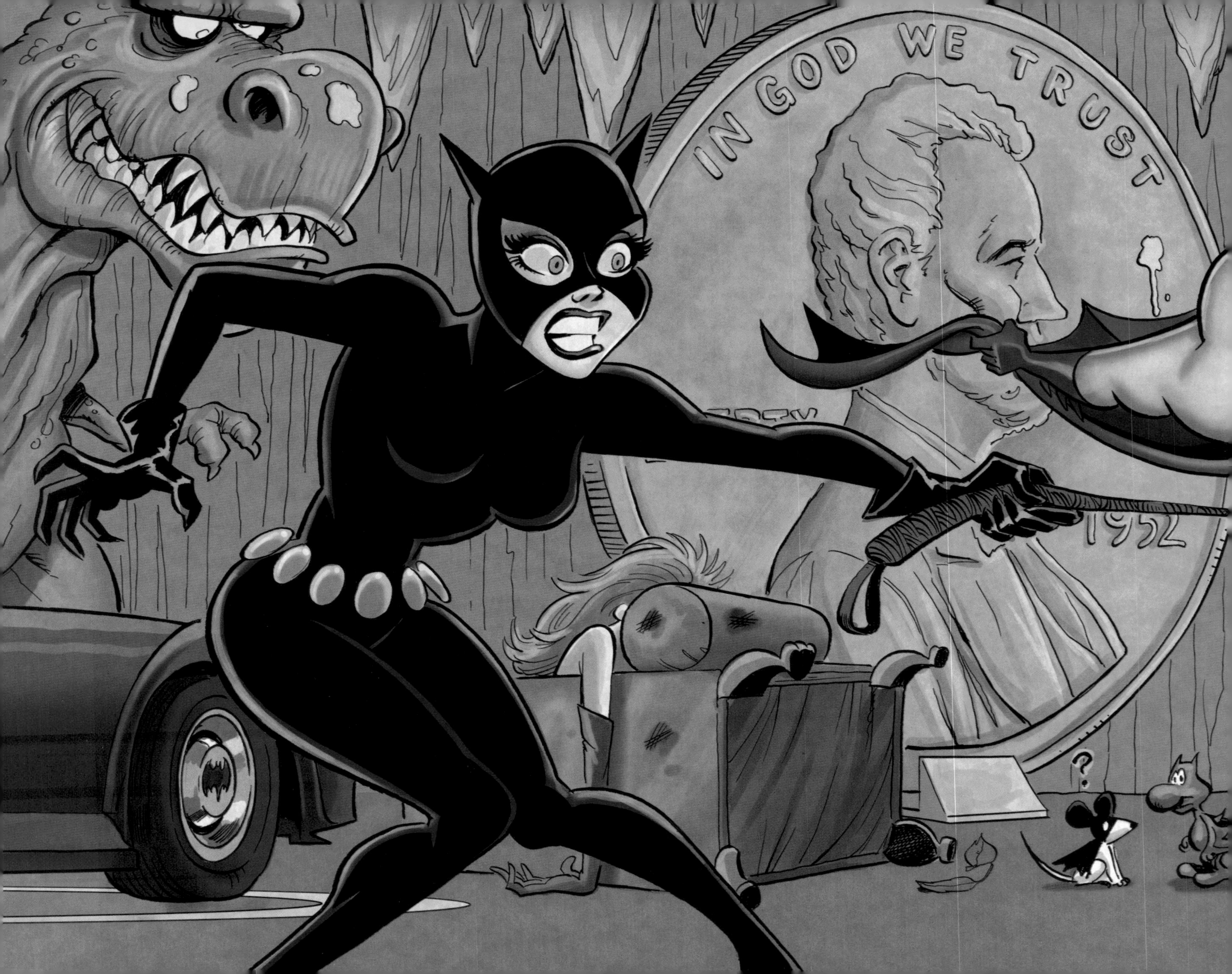
IN GOD WE TRUST
1952
?

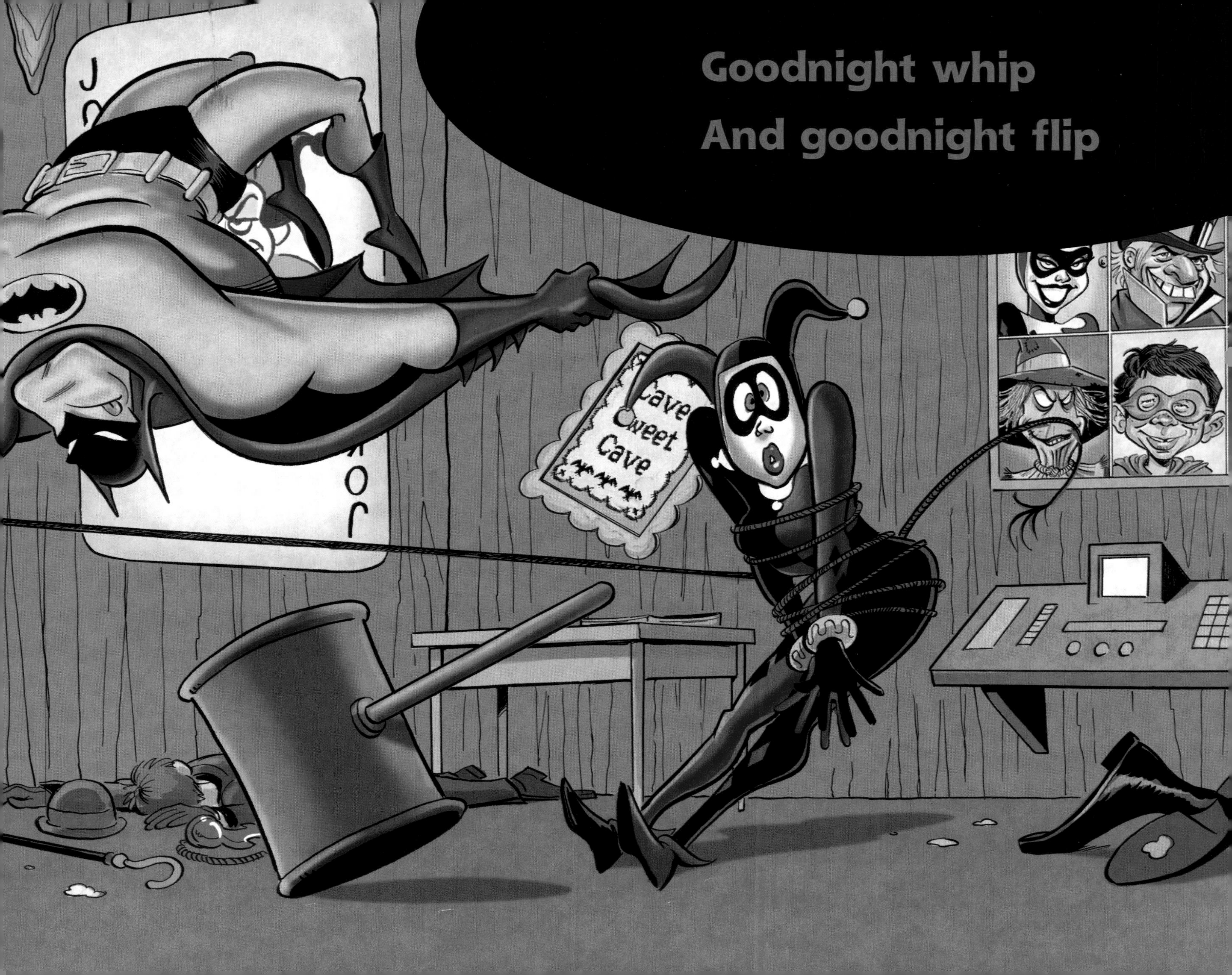
Goodnight whip
And goodnight flip

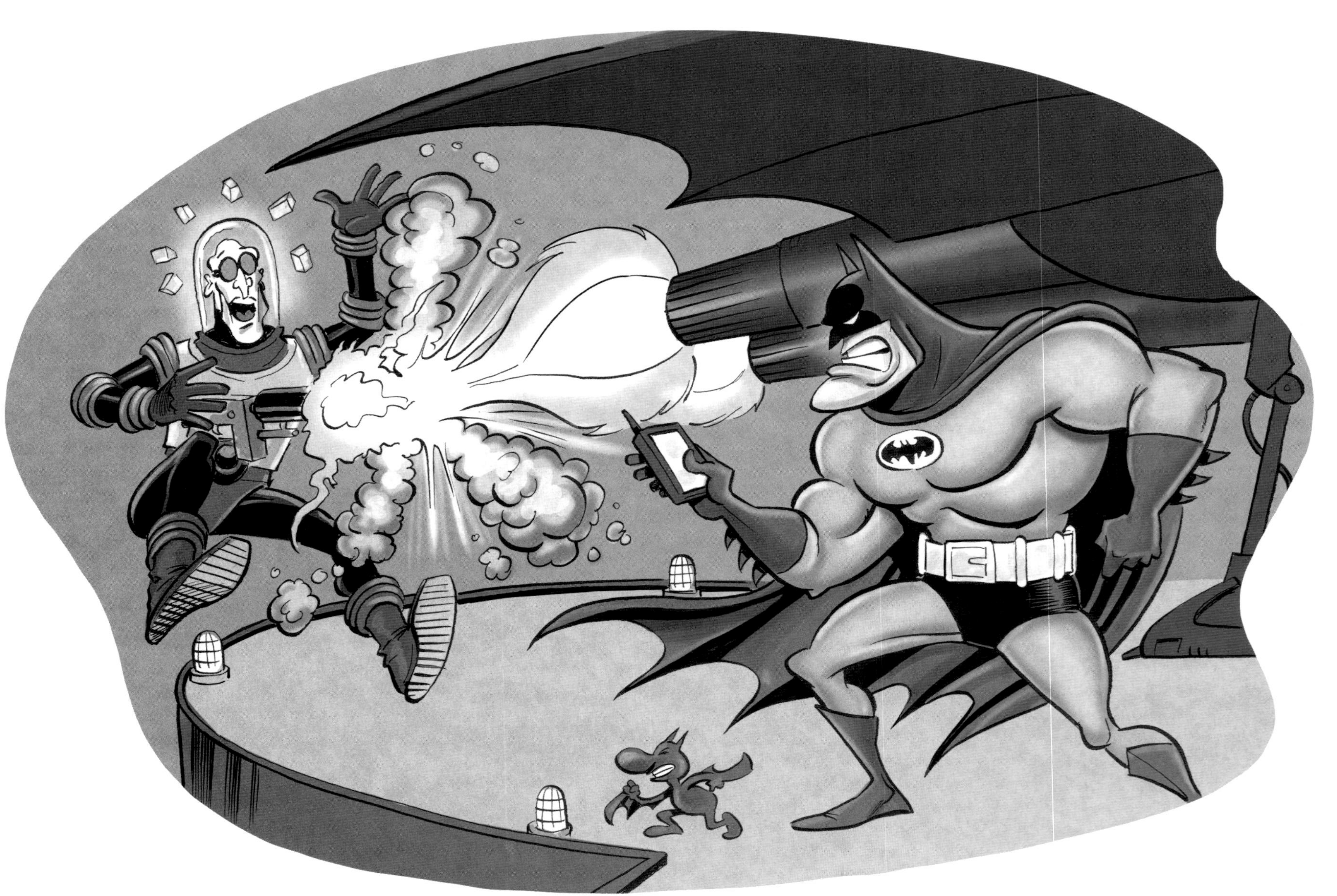

Goodnight giant jet

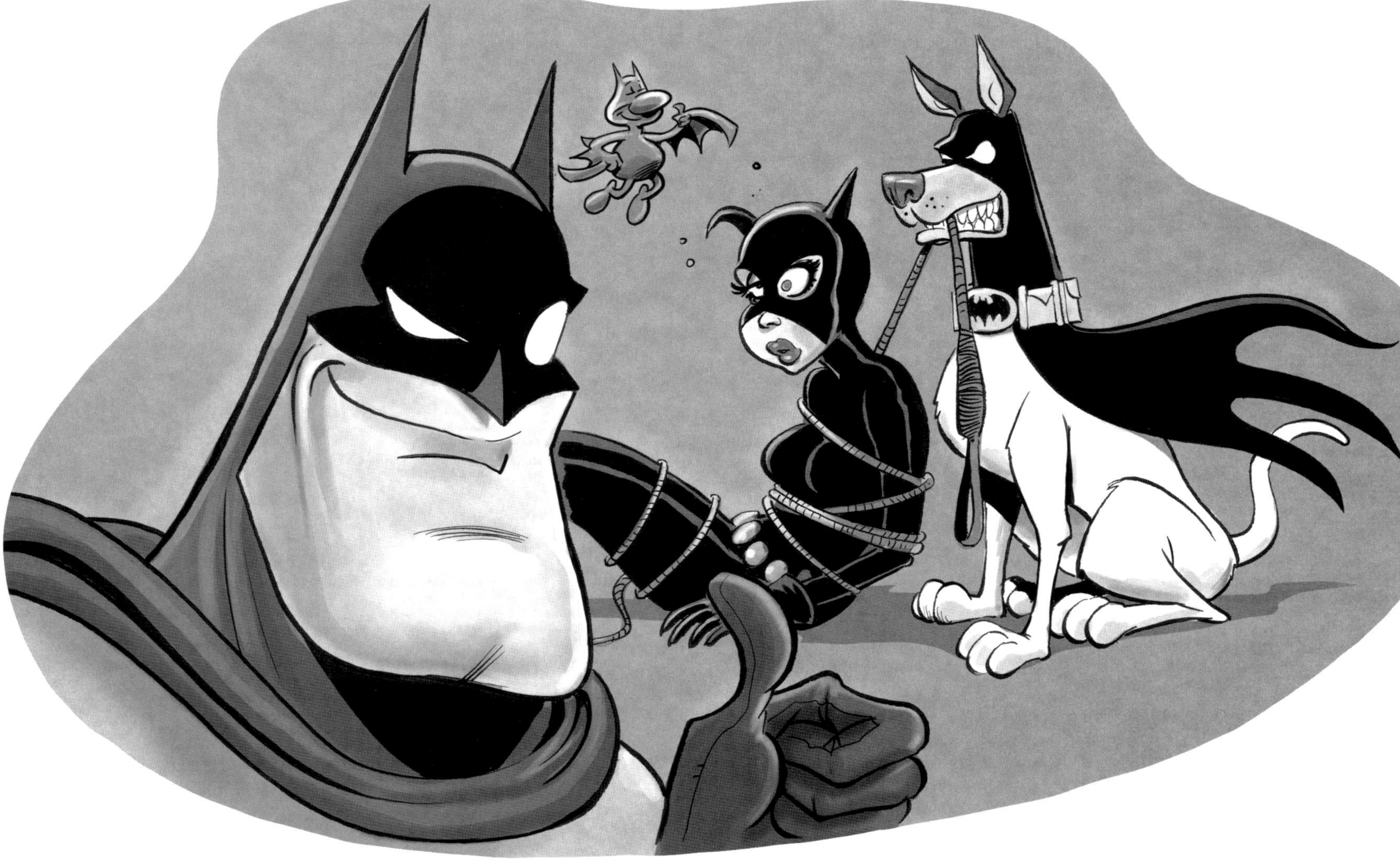

And goodnight pet

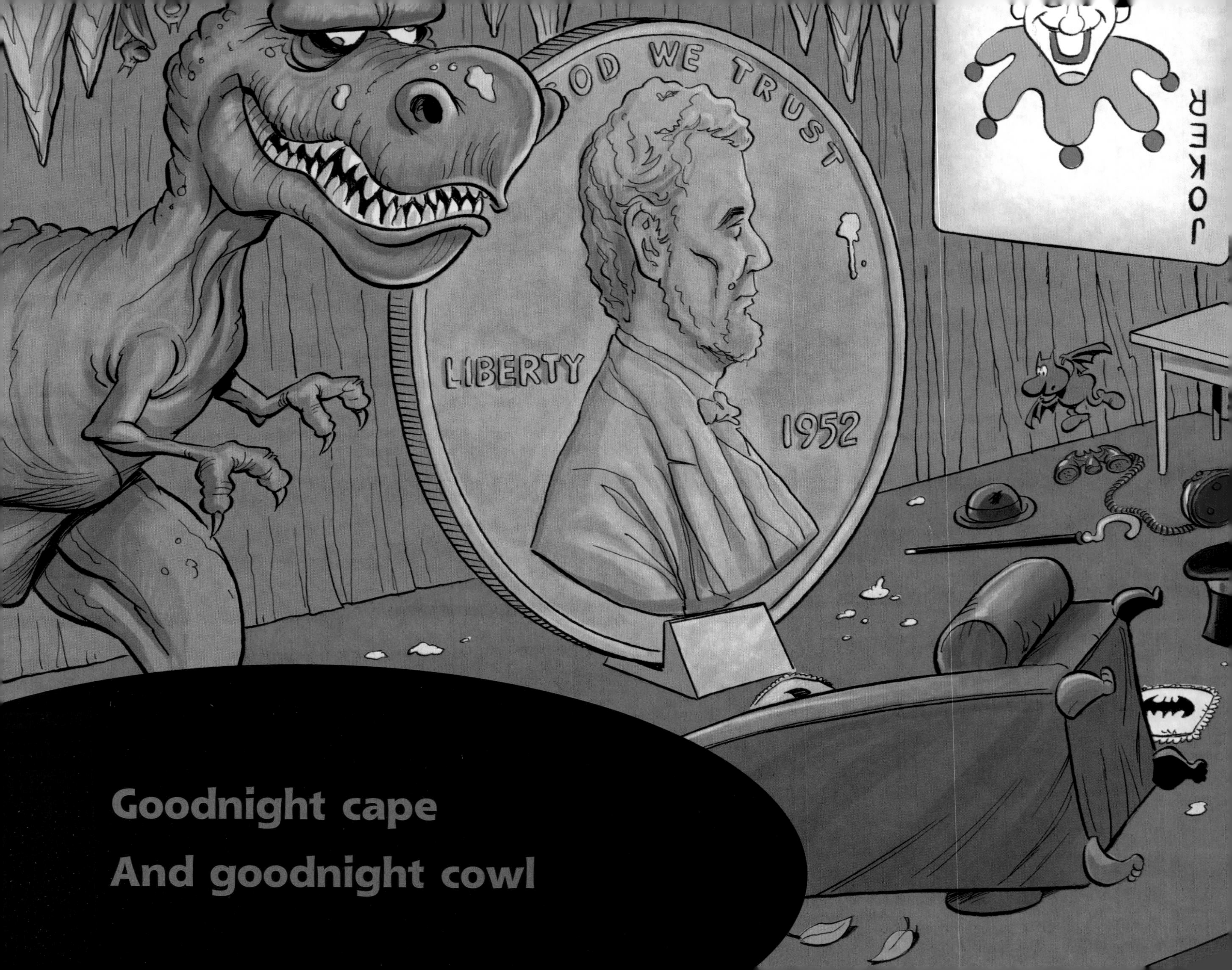
LIBERTY
1952

Goodnight cape
And goodnight cowl

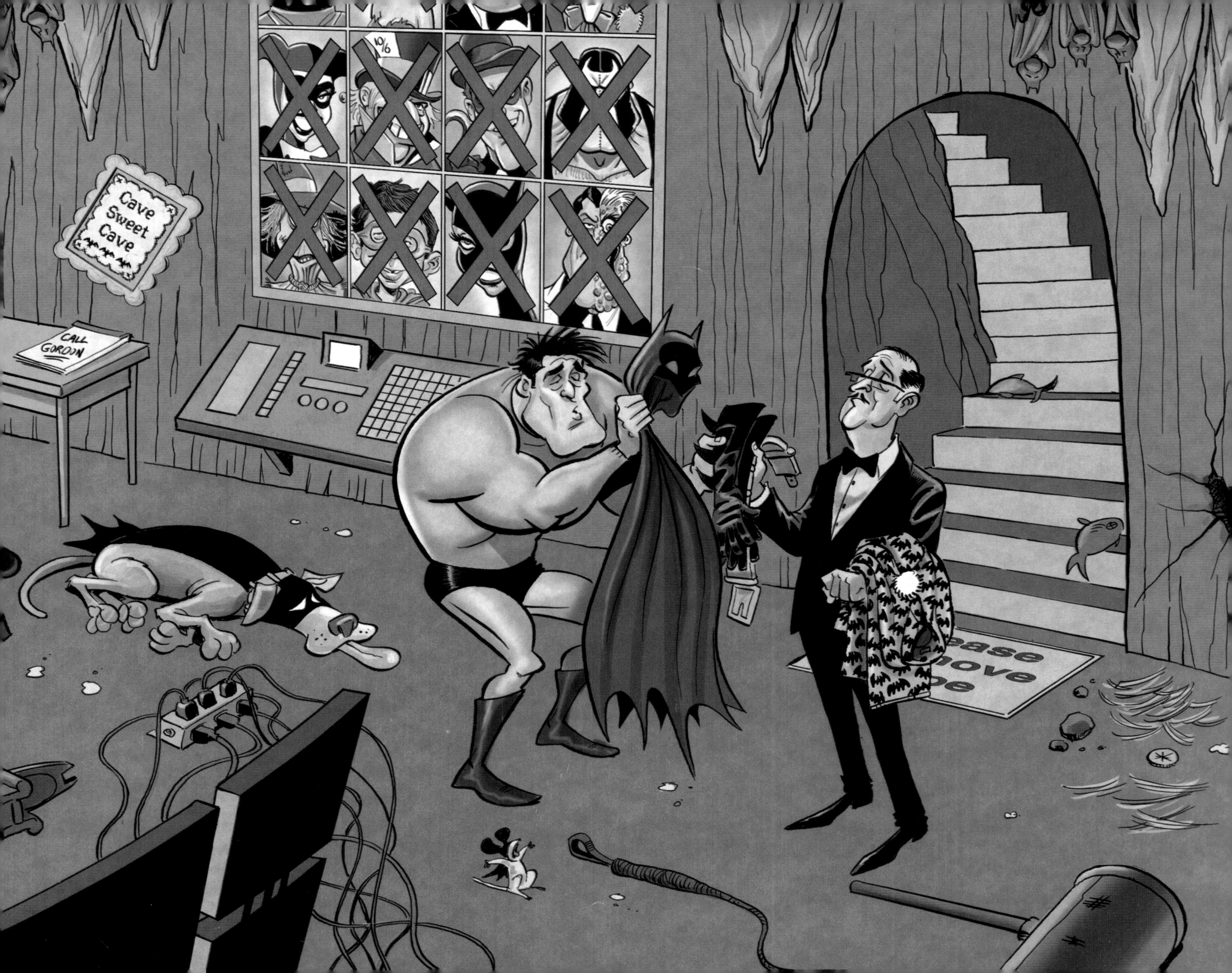
10/6
Cave Sweet Cave
CALL GORDON

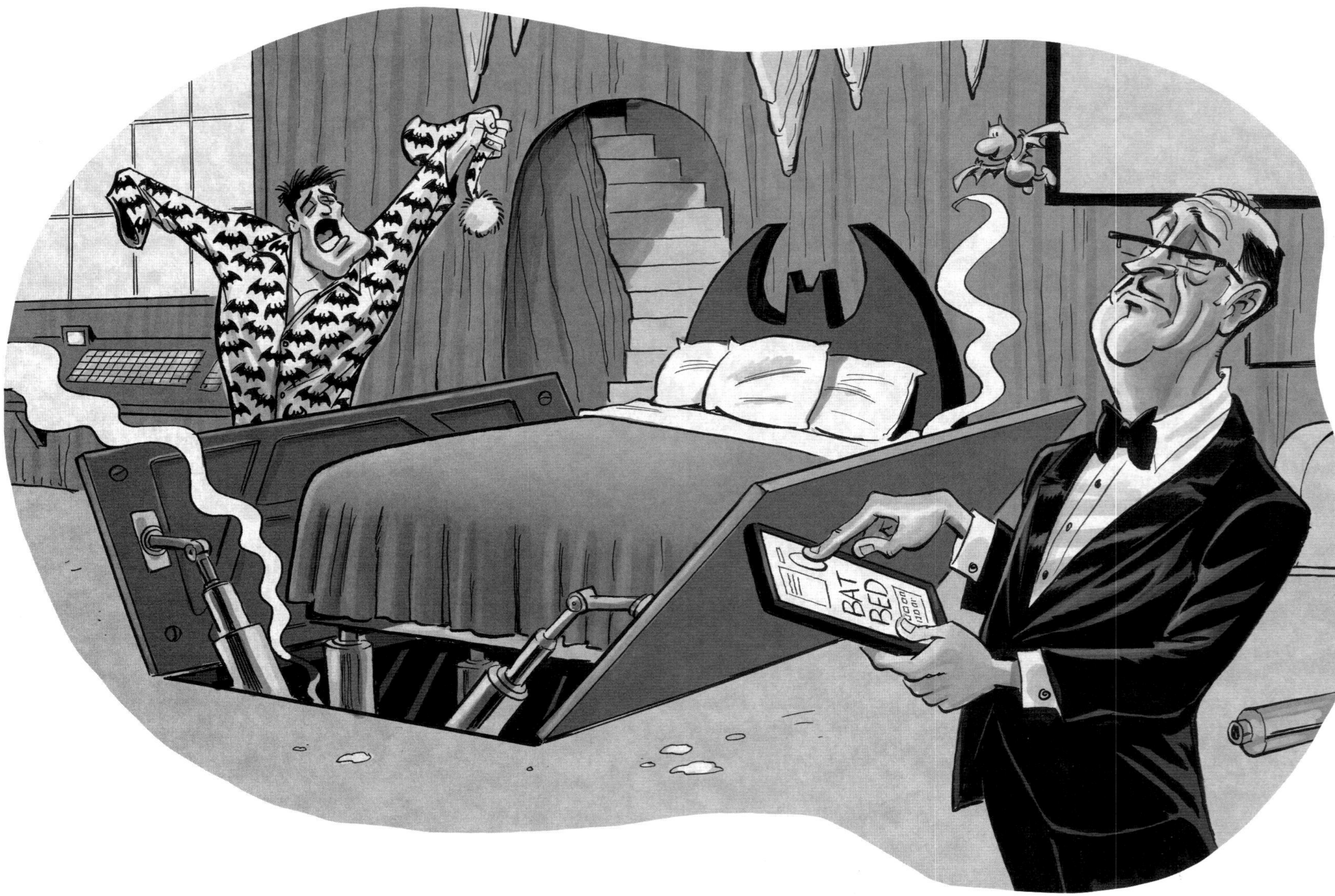
BAT
BED

Goodnight dear Alfred

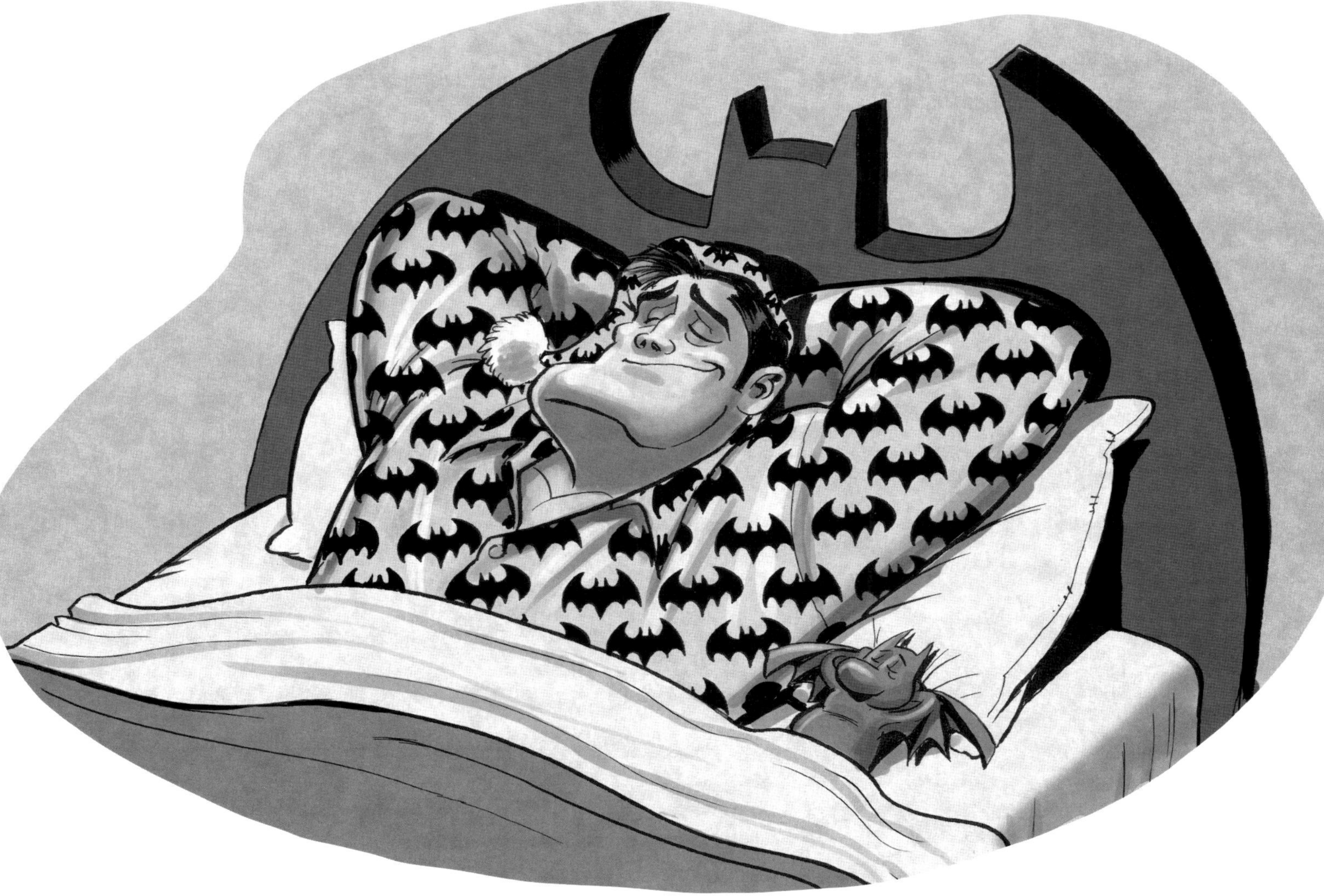

Goodnight scowl

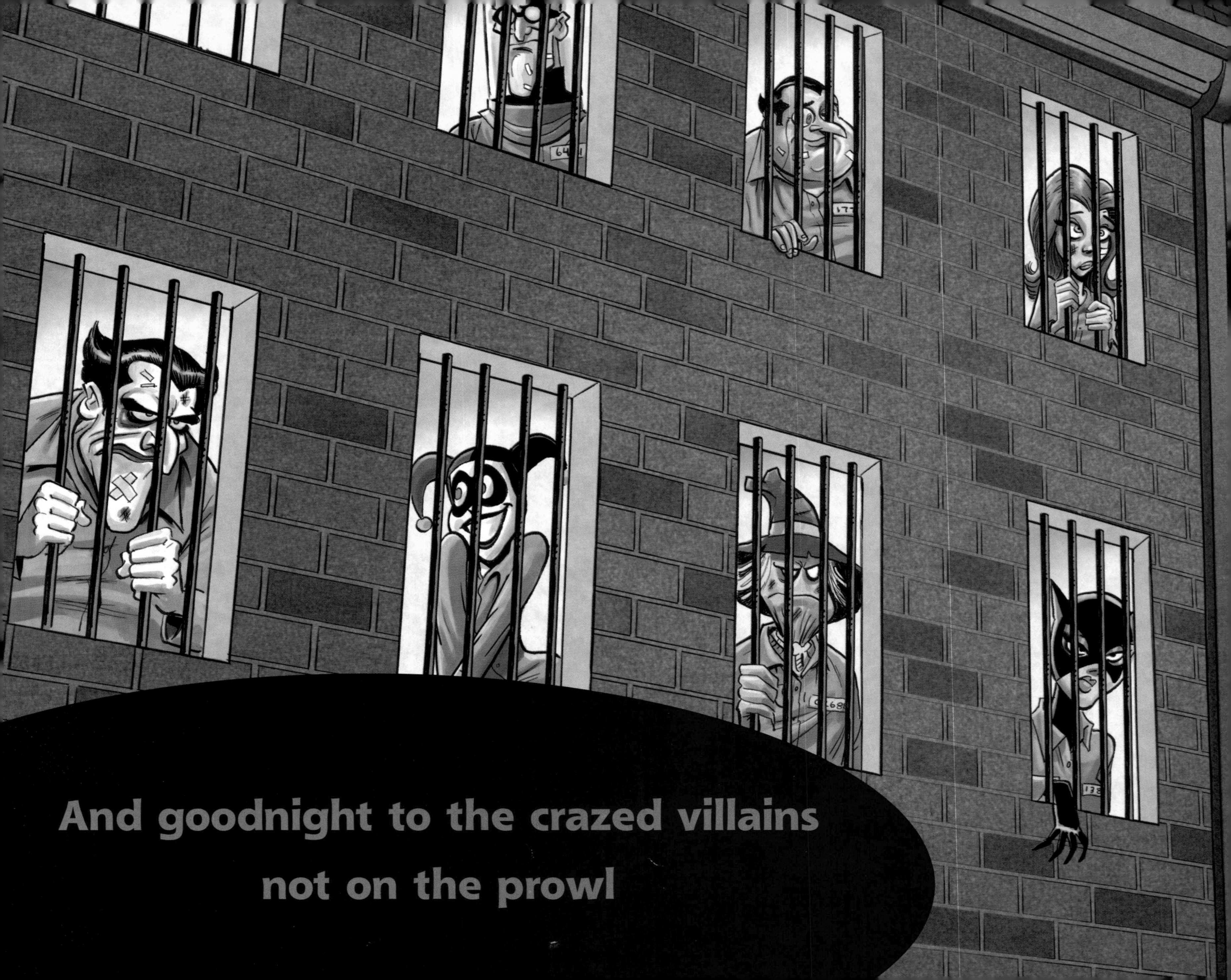

And goodnight to the crazed villains
not on the prowl

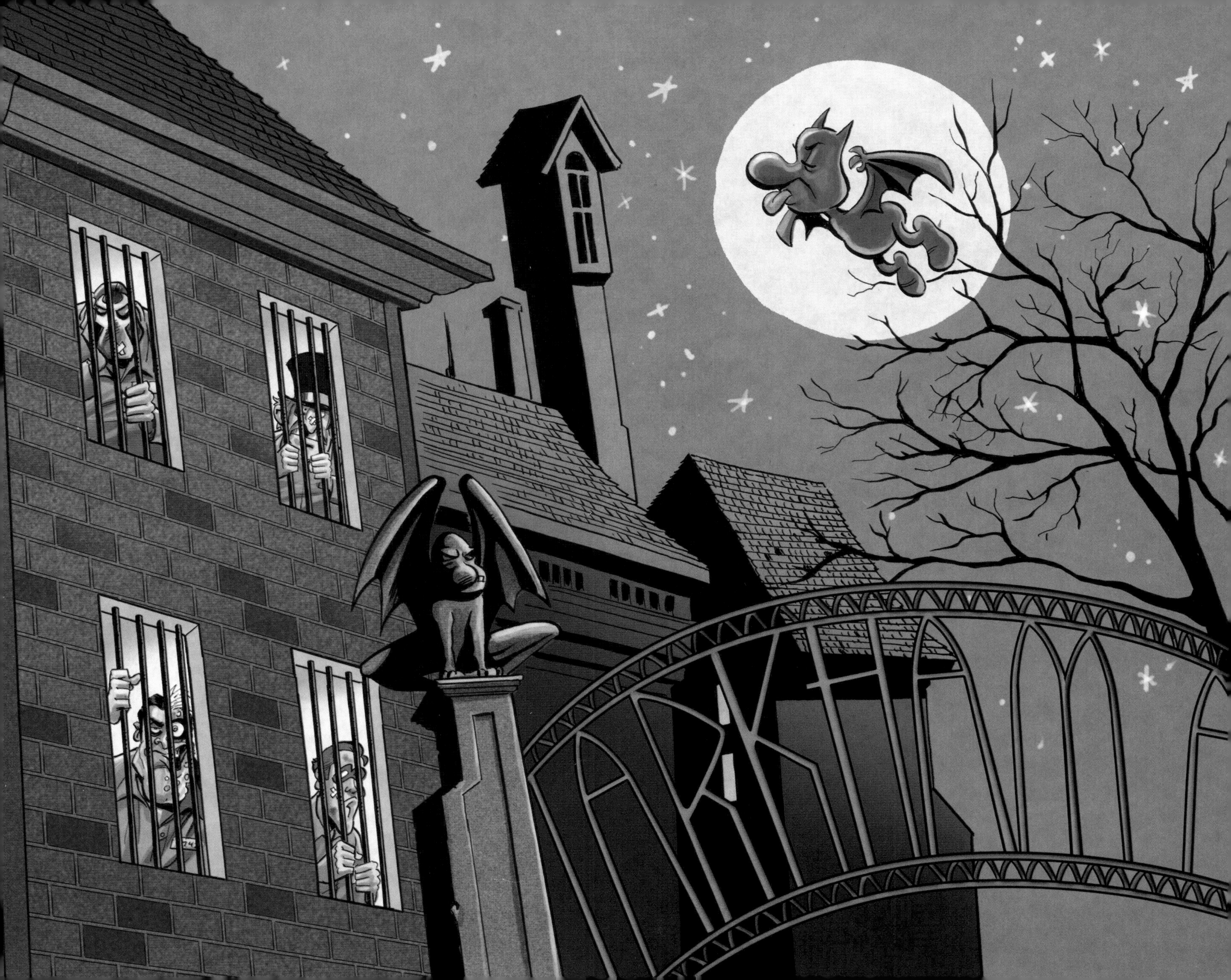

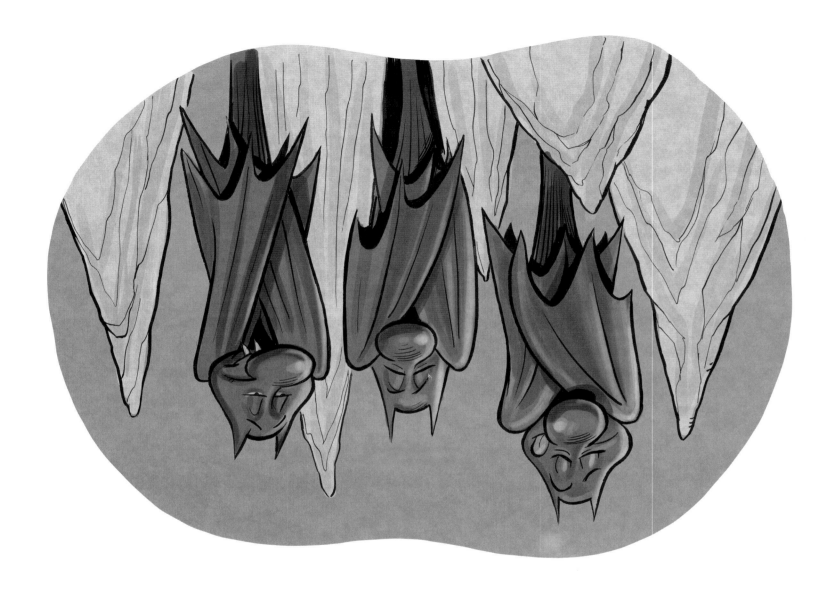

Goodnight bats

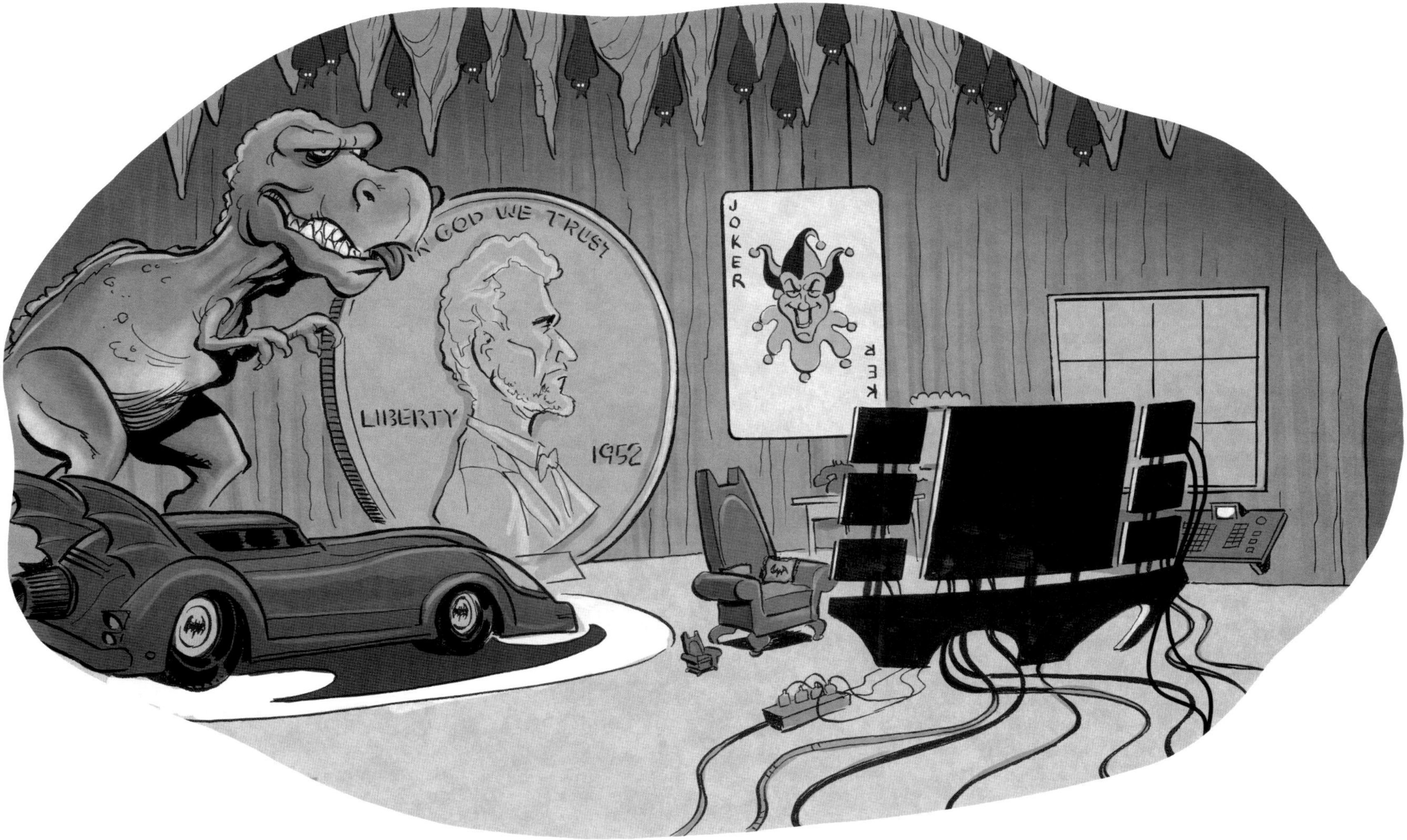

IN GOD WE TRUST
LIBERTY
1952
JOKER

Goodnight lair

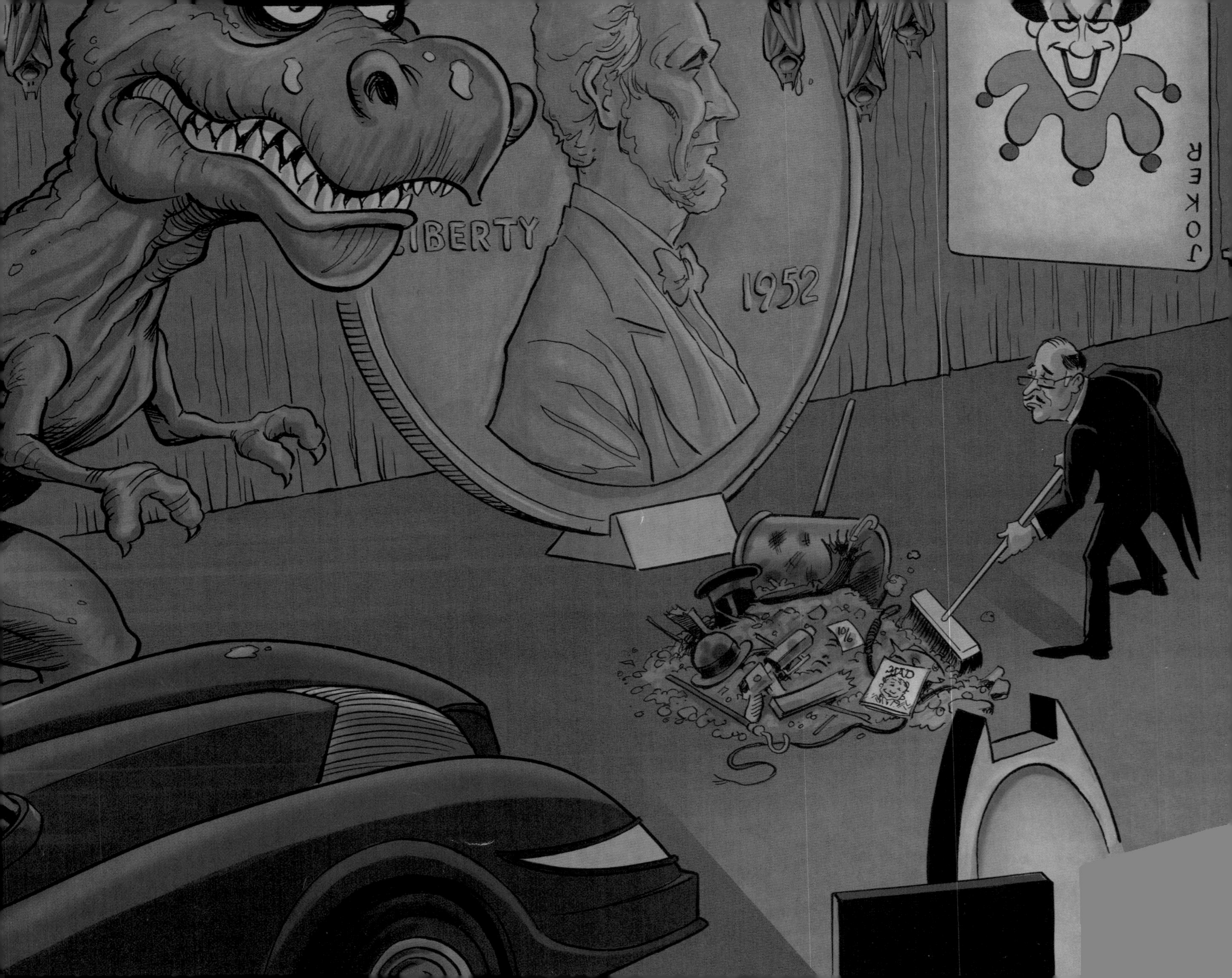
LIBERTY
1952
JOKER

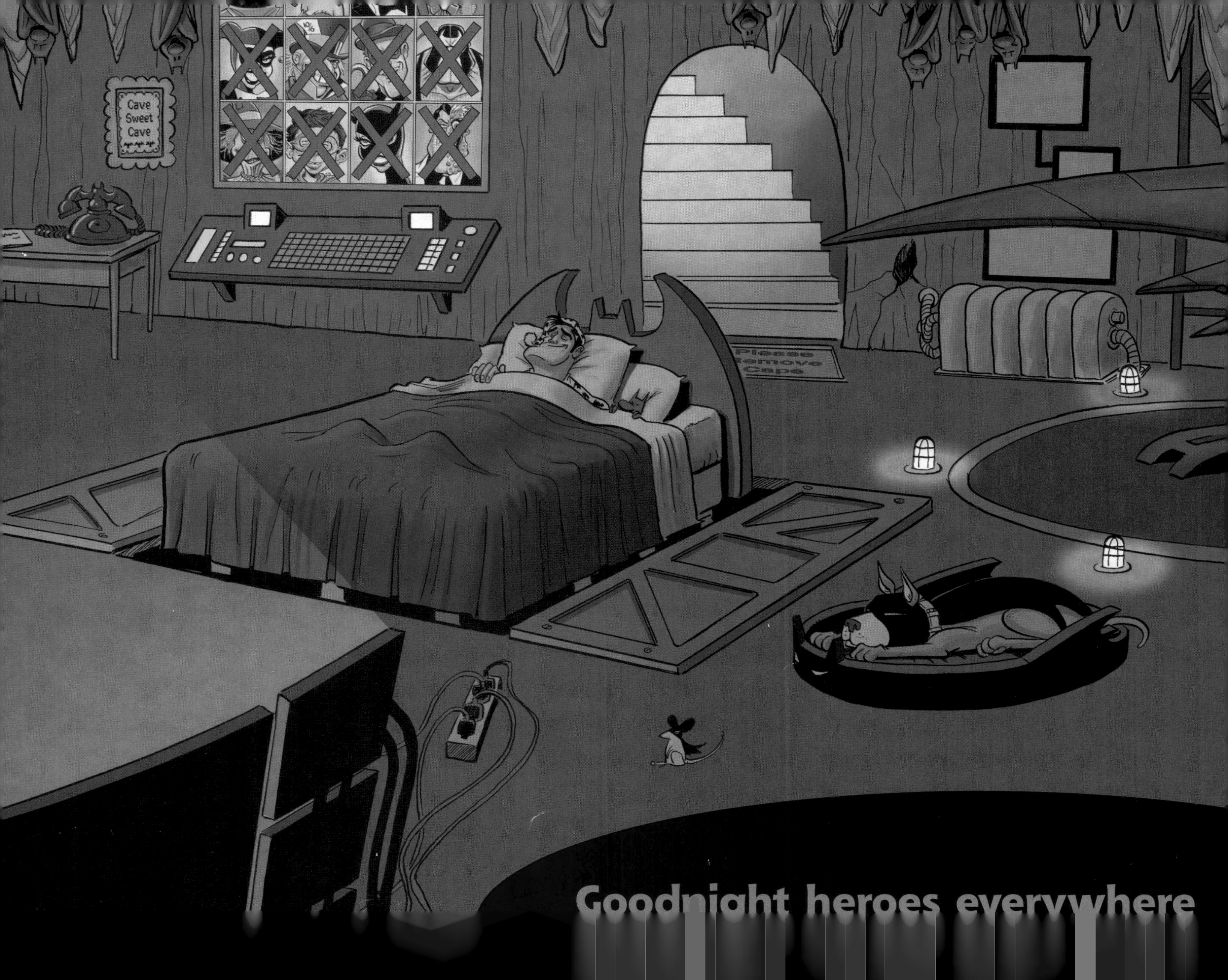
Cave Sweet Cave
Please Remove Cape

Goodnight heroes everywhere

MAD BOOKS

William M. Gaines Founder
John Ficarra Senior VP & Executive Editor
Charlie Kadau, Joe Raiola Senior Editors
Dave Croatto Editor
Jacob Lambert Associate Editor
Sam Viviano VP – Art & Design
Ryan Flanders Associate Art Director
Patricia Dwyer Assistant Art Director

ADMINISTRATION

Diane Nelson President
Dan DiDio and Jim Lee Co-Publishers
Geoff Johns Chief Creative Officer
Amit Desai Senior VP – Marketing & Global Franchise Management
Nairi Gardiner Senior VP – Finance
Sam Ades VP – Digital Marketing
John Cunningham VP – Content Strategy
Anne DePies VP – Strategy Planning & Reporting
Don Falletti VP – Manufacturing Operations
Lawrence Ganem VP – Editorial Administration & Talent Relations
Alison Gill Senior VP – Manufacturing & Operations
Hank Kanalz Senior VP – Editorial Strategy & Administration
Jay Kogan VP – Legal Affairs
Derek Maddalena Senior VP – Sales & Business Development
Jack Mahan VP – Business Affairs
Dan Miron VP – Sales Planning & Trade Development
Nick Napolitano VP – Manufacturing Administration
Carol Roeder VP – Marketing
Eddie Scannell VP – Mass Account & Digital Sales
Courtney Simmons Senior VP – Publicity & Communications
Jim (Ski) Sokolowski VP – Comic Book Specialty & Newsstand Sales
Sandy Yi Senior VP – Global Franchise Management

For Carter and Evan, from Dad

Published by MAD Books. An imprint of E.C. Publications, Inc.,
1325 Avenue of the Americas, New York, NY 10019.
A Warner Bros. Entertainment Company.

Printed in Mexico. First Printing.

ISBN: 978-1-4012-7010-0

Library of Congress Cataloging-in-Publication Data is available

Though Alfred E. Neuman wasn't the first to say "A fool and his money
are soon parted," here's your chance to prove the old adage right —
subscribe to MAD! Simply call 1-800-4-MADMAG to order!

Visit MAD online at: www.madmagazine.com